AUSSIE TALK

Published by Brolga Publishing Pty Ltd
ABN 46 063 962 443
PO Box 12544
A'Beckett St
Melbourne, VIC, 8006
Australia

email: markzocchi@brolgapublishing.com.au

All rights reserved. No part of this publication may be reproduced, stored in a retrieval system or transmitted in any form or by any means electronic, mechanical, photocopying, recording or otherwise without prior permission from the publisher.

Copyright © 2012 Paul Bugeja

National Library of Australia Cataloguing-in-Publication entry
Author: Bugeja, Paul.
Title: Aussie talk : Australian slang-uage : sayings, slang and idiom, the Aussie way / Paul Bugeja.
ISBN: 9781922036834 (pbk.)
Subjects: Australianisms. English language--Australia--Terms and phrases.
Dewey Number: 427.994

Printed in China
Cover design by David Khan
Typeset by Wanissa Somsuphangsri

BE PUBLISHED

Publish Through a Successful Australian Publisher
National Distribution & International Distribution to
the United Kingdom, North America &
Sales Distribution to South East Asia
Email: markzocchi@brolgapublishing.com.au

Aussie Talk

Australian 'Slanguage' –

Sayings, Slang and Idiom the Aussie Way

Paul Bugeja

Dedication

This one is for the Ogiers, Selma and Pattie,
Two of my besties
Who are the duck's nuts when it comes to friendship,
Have blood worth bottling,
And whom I have little reason to believe that either of them would ever come the raw prawn with me.

Dedication

This one is for the Daters, Saina and Artie,
two of my besties
Who are the ducks I turn to when it comes to friendship,
have blood worth spilling,
And without whom I have no reason to believe that either of them would ever come the raw prawn with me.

Contents

Introduction..9
Greetings & Farewells....................................13
Compliments..17
Insults..23
Exclamations/Expressions of Surprise...............39
Threats, Warnings & Taunts............................49
Descriptions: Character/Personal/Emotional....57
Sport...65
At the Pub/Social Gatherings.........................73
The Mating Game/ Sexology...........................79
Toilet Humour..87
Time and Space..91
Online Acronyms..97
General: All the rest!.....................................99

Introduction

Slang, and the sayings and expressions it is contained within, is an integral component of a country's national identity, and Aussies, as we all know, are no exception.

Not only have we imported and adapted more general 'international' slang to our own vernacular, but there also exists an entire body of idiom that has arisen as we have developed as a nation.

Many of us use this slang every day—some of us, it must be said, more than others—and half the time we might be oblivious to the fact that we are letting it fly mid-conversation.

In fact, 'Strine', as it has come to be known, is deeply imprinted into who we are and how we communicate, philologically branding us as 'Aussies' whenever we open our mouths.

However, before you delve any further, I must offer something of a caveat…

A smallish portion of the content of this book is what I would call 'time-capsule material'—language that should be buried deep and only brought out as a way of gaining an historical snapshot of how we communicated at a certain point in time.

Thus, there are words and sayings no longer in popular use but which I have included even thought they will be deemed as politically incorrect or lacking in tack or sensibility by today's standards.

To leave some of these 'old-school', pre-political-correctness-era sayings out would, I believe, be something of a disservice to the development of our nation linguistically, socially and philosophically.

It would be burying our head in the sand of our past.

Quite simply, we can't ignore this past, good and bad, and given that language is the main medium for passing history on, both in oral and written form, it is imperative we represent it truthfully.

Because of this, I have included within the collection some of the less politically correct language and hope it will be read within an historical context - seen through the prism of recording such sayings and language for posterity rather than their inclusion as hurtful reminders of somewhat derogatory language from days gone by.

Introduction

I also wish to stress that this tome should not be mistaken as the absolutely, one hundred per cent, 'everything under one roof' book on all things Strine.

In fact I have no doubt some readers will feel hard done by when they find what they see as potentially glaring omissions—favourite sayings they feel should have made it into this book, and probably were under consideration but that were culled in the editing process.

My advice to you—don't get angry, get them to me!

I want to hear from every 'Tom, Dick or Mary ' who feels aggrieved that their favourite 'dinky-di' Aussie saying has not been included so that they can be considered for any future editions.

Email any suggestions to:
aussieslangpb@gmail.com

Enjoy this collection. I'm sure it will evoke smiles, laughs, nods of recognition and the occasional embarrassed grimace. Overall, it is my hope that it is taken as intended, as a light-hearted look at 'Australian Slanguage'

Paul Bugeja

Greetings & Farewells

Few would argue that 'G'day' is the most world-renowned Aussie greeting, and there would be few Australians who have not used it at one time or another.

Aside from this standard there are a multitude of others, farewells too, most of which don't require explanation, as their meanings are self-evident, although some might be a little more obscure than others or have particular slants...

A

(I was) **About to send out a search party:** Addressing someone who arrives late to a rendezvous (usually with a liberal dose of sarcasm)

B

Back in two shakes (of a willy): I'll be back very soon

Be good or be good at it

C

Catch ya'; also catch ya' later and catch ya' later when your legs are straighter

Come in spinner: Let's go

Cop-you-later

D

Don't be a stranger

Don't do anything I wouldn't do

Greetings & Farewells

H

Haven't seen you in donkeys/yonks: Said to someone you haven't seen in a long time

Hello, here's trouble

How are you me old china?

Howzit Garn'?

I

I wouldn't be dead for quids (reply to greeting)

If you can't be good, be careful

I'm off...
- Like a bride's nightie
- Like a bucket of prawns in the sun
- Like a fish milkshake
- Like a hooker's nightie
- Like a Jewish foreskin

- Like a robber's dog
- Like a three-day-old bucket of prawns
- Like the clappers
- To see a man about a dog

I'm shooting through

It's been a long time between drinks

L

Let's hit the road

Look what the cat dragged in

S

Saw your light on, thought I'd drop in

See you 'round like a rissole

Seeya' later alligator

'Sgarnon: What's going on?

W

We have to stop meeting like this

What's the John Dory: rhyming slang for **what's the story?**

Compliments

Australians are renowned both at home and abroad for their easy-going, friendly nature, although at times we tend to suffer the oft-discussed 'Tall Poppy Syndrome', which means compliments may come less often than not...

When they do come, they may sound a little pithy at first before they are recognised for what they are—good-natured, sometimes tongue-in-cheek, compliments- Aussie-style!

A

A better man never stood in two shoes: A great man; also used as a plea by someone to plead that they are a good person

(The) **Ant's pants:** The best there is

B

(The) **Bee's knees:** The best available *(origin: bees carry pollen on the mid-segments of their legs)*

(The) **Best thing since sliced bread:** A simple thing that is really good

(He/she is a) **Bit of a numpty:** An idiot but often used endearingly amongst friends

(A) **Bit rough around the edges:** A handsome man who is very masculine or macho and not overdressed or over-coiffed ie not a SNAG (sensitive new age guy)

(Her/his) **Blood is worth bottling:** A very precious person

Bright-eyed and bushy-tailed: Full of energy; exuberant

Built like a brick shit-house: Solidly built, generally male

Compliments

C

(That's/she's/he's a) **Corker: Striking**; outstanding; brilliant

(He/she) **Could kick the arse off an emu:** Extremely fit

(She/he/it is to) **Die for:** Excellent; very attractive

(It's the) **Duck's nuts:** As good as it gets

F

(As) **Fit as a Mallee bull:** Someone extremely strong and fit

Fully sick/sik mate: Amazing

G

(As) **Game as a piss ant:** Very brave

Gift of the gab: Possessing the ability to talk confidently and with authority in a very convincing fashion

Goes like the clappers: Works hard or moves very quickly; when 'she' is added to this saying, it becomes a reference to a sexually voracious or sexually skilled woman

Going hammer and tongs: Energetically

Going off like a frog in a sock: Frenetically; vigorously; with much effort

(He/she's) **Got balls:** Brave; courageous; prepared to take a risk (under the false assumption that men are bravest because they have testicles!)

I

(Something/Someone is) **In good nick:** In good shape; in good health; in good condition

L

Live/Run on the smell of an oily rag: Not requiring

much money or many resources to survive or function

M

Make/Made a good fist of it: Try/Tried as hard as possible to do something

N

No flies on him/her: Thinks and/or acts quickly

Not backwards in coming forward: Very confident and quite often vocal about it

P

(I'm not trying to/I wouldn't) **Piss in your pocket:** Complimenting someone genuinely, without motive

Pretty spiffy: Excellent or particularly fine physical appearance of someone/thing

S

Scrubs up well: Makes an effort to dress well and looks good as a consequence

(Could) **Sell ice to the Eskimos:** Possesses the gift

of the gab (see above), but particularly convincing in the most unlikely scenario

She runs like a dream: A vehicle (most often) or other item that runs perfectly without issue

Sparking on all fours/cylinders: Working well or efficiently or at its peak

Straight to the pool room: A highly-prized item that should be on display for all to see

Insults

Far more often than complimenting each other, Aussies love to throw in their 'two bob's worth' of criticism when they feel it's due, giving as good as they get in terms of one upmanship in any duel of words.

It will therefore, no doubt, come as little surprise that there are almost five times as many insults as compliments in this collection!

Some are designed to truly insult or stir up trouble, others to generate a laugh, and many are, let's say, somewhat 'vivid' linguistically!

Sadly, some of the more colourful expressions are rarely used today… maybe we should bring them back into vogue?

A

Acting the goat: Being particularly foolish

Act your age, not your shoe size: Stop acting foolishly or childishly

Away with the pixies/fairies: Not with it or paying attention

B

(To) **Bag someone:** To put someone down

Barmy as a bandicoot: Insane; acting in an erratic fashion

Bash somebody's ear: Talk too much

(He/she has) **Been hit with the ugly stick/fugly stick:** A really ugly person

(A) **Bit airy fairy:** Light on detail, intelligence or gravity

(A) **Bit on the nose:** Not quite right; food that has gone bad; could indicate suspicion of some kind of corruption

(A) **Bit rough around the edges:** Unconventional or unskilled socially

Insults

(It's a) **Bit shonky/dodgy:** Disreputable; a question mark over authenticity or legality

(A) **Bit slow on the uptake:** Doesn't comprehend something as quickly as others

(It's a) **Bloody brothel:** A room or place that is extremely messy or dirty

(He/she/it) **Bore the pants off me:** Tedious in the extreme

Boring as batshit: Really boring

Bright as a two-watt globe: Simpleminded

(A) **Brick short of a load:** Simpleminded

(She/he's a) **Broken packet of biscuits:** Fine in appearance on the outside, but messed up emotionally

Built like the side of a house: Larger or overweight person, most often aimed at females

Bullshit artist: Liar; conman/woman

Butter wouldn't melt in your mouth: Very prim and proper; possessing a cool demeanour

C

Champagne tastes on a beer budget: Likes the good things in life but doesn't have the budget to maintain such

Carry on like a... —To make an unnecessary fuss or behave in a dramatic manner
- Chook with its head cut off
- Pork chop
- Two bob watch

(She/he) **Couldn't...**—Weak; cowardly; a poor fighter
- Fight your way out of a wet paper bag
- Go two rounds with a revolving door
- Knock the skin off a rice pudding

(He/she) **Couldn't drive a rusty nail up a dead dog's arse:** Completely useless

(She/he) **Could talk under wet cement with a mouth full of marbles:** Very talkative

(She/he) **Couldn't lie straight in bed:** Very dishonest

(He/she) **Couldn't organise a...**—Useless or totally disorganised or incapable
- Chook raffle in a country pub
- Piss up in a brewery
- Screw in a brothel

Insults

(She/he is as) **Crooked as a dog's hind leg:** Dishonest

(He/she is as) **Cunning/Crazy as a shit-house rat:** Extremely sly or underhanded

D

Done up like a pet lizard: To be overdressed

Don't be such a wet blanket: Don't put a dampener on things; stop being a spoilsport

Don't laugh, your face might crack: Stop being so serious

Don't just stand there like a stunned mullet: Do something; take action; get to it

Don't pick your nose or your head might cave in: How stupid can you be? (brainless)

Dull as a month of Sundays: Boring

Dumb as dog shit: Stupid

(A) **Face…**—Ugly
- Like a bashed in biscuit tin
- Like a smacked arse (also used for un unattractive momentary look of surprise or shock?)
- Only a mother could love—Self explanatory

F

(He/she) **Fell out of the ugly tree:** Very unattractive person

A few...short of...—Of low intelligence
- A few french fries short of a happy meal
- A few palings short of a fence
- A few sandwiches/sangers short of a picnic
- A few stubbies short of a sick pack

(A) **Few 'roos loose in the top paddock:** Irrational; a little mad

Insults

(To) **Flake out:** Breaking a commitment

(As) **Flash as a rat with a gold tooth:** Overdressed

All froth and no beer: Lacking substance

(As) **Funny as a...**—Not remotely comical
- Fart in a spacesuit
- Fart in an elevator
- Fart in a sleeping bag
- Fart in a phone booth
- Hat full of assholes

G

(She/he would) **Go to the opening of a chip packet:** Someone who is an over-socialiser; who would attend any kind of social gathering to be 'seen' no matter how insignificant the event is

Going through life with the porch-light dim: Not very intelligent

Gone 'round the bend: Gone mad

Gone to the dogs: Something that has gone badly wrong

Aussie Talk

Hang around like a bad smell: Someone who can't take the hint they aren't wanted

Hang shit on someone: Pick at someone's faults

Have tickets on yourself: Think you are better than you actually are

(A) **Head like a robber's dog:** Ugly

I

I didn't wake you, did I?: Sarcastic way of getting someone's attention, pointing out that they should be paying attention or aren't doing their assigned job or task

It was a dog act: Condemning someone's malicious or malevolent action

I've seen a better head on a glass of beer: Ugly

I've seen better legs on a table: Less than shapely legs of a female

Lights are on but nobody's home: Stupid

Like a mad woman's breakfast: Very disorganised

Like watching paint dry: Boring

(A) **Load of old cobblers:** Lies

Look like death warmed up: Unwell

Look like something the cat's dragged in: Unkempt; dishevelled

Look like a train wreck: Of terrible appearance

Lower than a snake's belly: Of low moral standing

M

Mad as a cut snake/meat axe: Angry; disturbed

(He/she) **made a real dog's breakfast out of it:** Really messed something up

Make a galah of yourself: Act foolish

(As) **mean as bird shit/cat's piss:** Really tight with money

More arse than class: More luck than style

More Chins than a Chinese phone book: Overweight

More front than Myers: Superficial; of little substance; also – cheeky; bold and forthright without justification ('Myers' referring to a major Australian department store)

Mutton done up as lamb: Overdressed; generally referring to an older woman trying to look young in terms of her clothing and make-up

N

Nasty piece of work: Of low or disreputable character

Not backwards in coming forward: Confident

Not much chop: Not much to speak of

Not my cuppa: Not interested in

Not the...—Simple-minded
- Brightest crayon in the box
- Brightest light on the Christmas tree
- Full quid
- Sharpest tool in the shed

Not what it's cracked up to be: Not as good as it has been made out to be

Not worth a brass razoo/a rat's arse: Worthless

Nothing between the ears: Stupid

Nothing to write home about: Plain; uninteresting

O

On the nose: Not right; going bad (food); morally questionable; possibly corrupt

Only has one oar in the water: Daydreamer

(All) **Over the shop like a madwoman's breakfast:** Scattered and unable to remain focussed

(She/he's an) **Oxygen thief:** Talks too much

P

(All) **Piss and vinegar:** Has a sour disposition and causes trouble

Pack of bludgers/galahs: Group of lazy types; no hopers

Piss it all against the wall: Waste something, usually money

R

Rough as guts: Unrefined; lacking social graces

Aussie Talk

Run around like a chook with its head cut off: Panic

S

(A) **Sandwich short of a picnic:**—Simple-minded

Say it, don't spray it: Someone talking excitedly; rapidly

Shadow of your former self: Someone who has changed dramatically and not for the best

(As) **Sharp as a billiard/bowling ball:** Stupid

Shit for brains: Someone who doesn't think much

Short arms, long pockets: Stingy with money

Short of numbers in the Upper House: Simple-minded (the Upper House referring to the Australian Parliament)

Slow as a wet week: Something that drags on seemingly endlessly

Snag short of a barbie/BBQ: Simple-minded

So far up yourself: Obnoxious; have a huge ego

Sticks out like dog's balls: Doesn't fit in

T

(As) Thick as…—Stupid
- A brick
- The dust on a public servant's in-tray
- Two planks

(He/she) Thinks his/her shit don't stink: To think you are better than you are

Thinks the sun shines out of his arse: Unjustifiably over-confident

Tickets on yourself: Over-confident

Tight as a fish's arse: Stingy with money

Two men and a dog: Poor attendance at an event of some kind

U

(As) Ugly as a hatful of arseholes: Very ugly

Ugly as sin: Very ugly

Up yourself: Over-confident; cocky

(As) Useful as lips on a chicken: Useless

(As) Useless as…—Ineffective or dysfunctional
- A hip pocket in a singlet
- A one-legged man in an arse kicking contest

- An ashtray on a motor bike
- Tits on a bull

V

(A) **Voice that could sour/curdle milk:** Particularly jarring voice

W

(Something is) **Wrong.com:** Wrong

(A) **Waste of space:** Useless

(As) **Weak as...**—Feeble
- A wet whistle
- Cat's piss
- Water

Were you born in a tent?—Close the door

Where'd you get your licence, on the back of a cornflakes packet?—Questioning someone's driving skills

Wouldn't know if his arse was on fire: Stupid

Wouldn't labour in childbirth: Lazy

(I) **Wouldn't piss on you if you were on fire:** I have no respect for you

(She/he) **Wouldn't shout if a shark bit her/him:** Stingy with money; will avoid buying a round of drinks

Wouldn't touch him/her with a ten foot pole: Disdain for someone, most often in relation to physical attraction

Wouldn't use him/her for shark bait: Such disrespect for someone that you wouldn't even throw them to the sharks

Wouldn't work in an iron lung: Extremely lazy

Wouldn't know his arse from his elbow: Doesn't have a clue

Y

You can't polish a turd: No matter how much you dress something up, it is still unworthy or useless

Aussie Talk

You must be the world's only living brain donor: Stupid

You pong: Smell bad

You've got a face on you like a smacked arse: Extremely ugly

You'd be late for your own funeral: Unpunctual

You're a Cadbury glass and a half: Simple-minded

You're piss-weak: Weak

Exclamations/ Expressions of Surprise

Australians are a declamatory mob—we say what we want, when we want and rarely hold back.

Whether a plea, knock-back or a more general throwaway line offered when we're caught out by a person or situation, we have at our disposal a wide range of cries, calls and other expressions.

A

(It's) **All over red rover:** It's finished

(A bit of) **A spin out:** Taken by surprise

All your Christmases have come at once: Extremely good luck has struck

Are you having a lend of me?—Are you lying?

Are you taking the mickey/the piss?—Are you trying to make a fool out of me?

B

Beg yours?—Please repeat what you said; did I really hear what you just said?

Belt up: Be quiet

Blimey/Crikey teddy: An expression of pent up emotions

Blow me down: Who would have thought?

Bob's you're uncle: As simple as that

Bugger me dead: Who would have thought?

Bugger that for a joke: Refusal to do or accept something

Buggered if I know: I have no idea

C

(I) **Couldn't give a continental:** I don't care

D

Dead-set: Absolutely

Do yourself a favour: Stop talking before you say something stupid

(I) **Don't give a brass razoo:** I don't care

Don't just stand there like a stunned mullet: Move it; do something

Don't bust a foofer valve: Don't overexert yourself (foofer valve=heart)

Done and dusted: Finished; completed

E

Even blind freddy could see it: It's very obvious

Every man/bastard and his dog: Everybody possible

Every Tom, Dick and Harry/Mary: Everyone

Excuse me for breathing: Response made when something you have said is dismissed out of hand

F

Fair crack of the whip: Be reasonable

Fair dinkum?—Really?; also, as an adjective in place of 'genuine' (See 'True Blue')

Fair go mate: Give me a chance; hold up

Fair shake/suck of the sauce bottle: I don't believe you; be reasonable

Flat out like a lizard drinking: Busy

For crying out loud: You can't be serious?

G

Get off the grass: I don't believe you

Get rooted: Get lost; go away

Give us a gander: Let me have a look

Give us a go: Let me have a try

Good onya': Well done (said with irony)

Exclamations/ Expressions of surprise

I

I don't give a rats: I don't care

I don't give a stuff: I don't care

K

Knock your socks off: Don't hold back; go for it

N

No worries/No wuckas/No wucken furries: That's fine; I'll take care of it

No drama: It's not a problem

Not on your nelly: Absolutely not

P

Pig's arse: I don't think so; no way

Pull the other one: Stop trying to deceive me; I don't believe you

Pull your finger out: Work harder; get to it

(You're) **Pulling my chain:** You can't be serious?

S

She'll be …—Everything will be ok
- Apples
- Right
- Sweet

Shit a brick: Damn

(The) **Shit's going to hit the fan:** There is going to be a lot of trouble

Shove that up your arse: Deal with that

Stiff bickies/cheddar: Too bad

Stone the crows: I can't believe it; I'm annoyed

Strike a light/me lucky: Who would have thought?

Exclamations/ Expressions of surprise

T

Tell him he's dreaming/You're dreaming: Whatever you might think, it's not going to go that way, if at all

That'd be right: That would be my bad luck

Too right: Absolutely

Tough titties: Too bad

True Blue: Absolutely; also, as an adjective in place of 'genuine' (see 'Fair Dinkum')

Turn it up: Don't lie to me

W

(This) **Will knock your socks off:** You will be surprised by this

Wake up Australia: Get with it

Well I'll be blowed: Who would have thought?

Whacko the diddlyo: Fantastic; brilliant

What a balls up: What a huge mistake

What a bobby dazzler: How wonderful

What a cack: How funny

What a load of cod's wallop/old cobblers: Nonsense

What a pearler: What a good one; how brilliant; that's spot on

What are ya'?—Who do you think you are?

What are ya' like?—Term of endearment when someone does something silly

What did your last slave die of?—Stop being so lazy; do it yourself

What do you think this is, bushweek?—Stop being lazy; get on with it

What's up his/her arse?—What is wrong with him/her?

Where's the fire?—Why are you in a rush?

Who's skinning this cat?—Who's in control of this situation?

Who's he when he's at home?—Aimed at someone who is big-noting themselves or who is particularly cocky

Wouldn't be dead for quids: Extremely happy to be alive

Exclamations/ Expressions of surprise

Wouldn't it rot your socks off?—Isn't it disappointing?

Wouldn't know him from a bar of soap: I have no idea who that is

Y

You drongo: Term of endearment when someone does something silly

You little beauty/ripper: Expresses excitement or happiness

You silly whacker: See 'you drongo'

You've got legs, haven't ya'?—Do it yourself

You're not wrong: You're right!

Threats, Warnings & Taunts

It's not that Aussies are necessarily aggressive as a people—but we certainly are 'up for it' when challenged and won't back down untill we feel the situation is resolved.

We will call out people when we feel it's right, challenge them when we're unhappy with their actions and send them packing with a mouthful of true-blue Strine if pushed to it.

A

Avago ya' mug: Used to incite a fight; a comeback after a taunt

B

Beat the living daylights/shits out of someone: Hurt someone badly

(I'll) **Belt the living suitcase out of ya':** I'll fight you and beat you up badly

Belt up: Quieten down; stop speaking

Bite your bum: Shut up

D

Don't get narky: Don't be irritated

Don't piss in my pocket: I don't want to hear your problems

(You've) **Done your dash:** Had all your chances

Don't come the raw prawn with me: Don't lie to me; don't try to deceive me

Don't play funny buggers with me: Stop skirting around the truth

F

Fed up to the back teeth: Can't take any more; I'm completely frustrated

F*ck you and the horse you rode in on: Aggressive dismissive retort

G

Get a black dog up ya': Get f*cked

Get a life: General taunt

Get off your bike/high horse: Stop acting in a superior manner

Get over yourself: Drop the attitude

Get up my goat: Get on my nerves

Get your arse into gear: Hurry up

Give a dog a bone: I don't believe you

Giving you the Jimmy Brits: rhyming slang for **give you the shits**; irritating

Go and stick your head up a dead bear's bum: Stop bothering me

Go and take a running jump at yourself: Get away from me

Go to buggery: Get away

H

Hope your balls turn into bicycle wheels and backpedal up your arse: General insult

Hope your chooks turn into emus and kick your dunny doors down: Wishing bad luck of the worst sort on someone

I

I'll have your guts for garters: Threat to inflict physical violence on someone

I'll knock your teeth so far down your throat you'll have to stick a toothbrush up your arse to clean your teeth: Threat to inflict physical violence on someone

I'm ropeable: Indicates extreme anger

M

May your ears turn into arseholes and shit on your shoulders: General taunt

Mind your own bee's wax: Mind your own business

P

Pull your head in: Stop talking or behaving in a certain (usually obnoxious) manner

Pull your finger out/socks up: Work harder; get moving

Put a cork in it/sock in it: Be silent; shut up

Put that in your pipe and smoke it: That's what I think; indicates the conversation is over

Put up your dooks: Let's fight

R

Rack off: Get out of here; move on

S

Shut your gob/bunghole: Stop talking

Stick that up your jumper and smoke it: A challenge: can you do better than that?

Stop dillydallying: Hurry up

Stop faffing around: Stop wasting time; stop avoiding doing something

Stop playing silly buggers/playing the goat: Stop fooling around

Suck it up (princess): Stop complaining and deal with a difficult situation

T

Take a chill pill: Stop stressing out

Tell someone who cares: I'm not interested in what you're saying

W

Was your father a glassmaker?—Move out of the way (I can't see through you)

What's your beef?—What is your problem?

(A) **wigwam for a goose's bridle:** A warning to mind one's business

Y

You havin' a go?—Are you making fun of me?

You're giving me the tom tits: rhyming slang for **you're giving me the shits**; you're irritating me

Z

Zip your lips: Keep quiet

Descriptions: Character/ Personal/Emotional

Whether we are describing our own emotional or physical state or what we think of someone or how we feel they look, there is a collection of 'expressive' and often very colorful descriptions at our disposal.

A warning: only read on if you won't be offended, as some of this language might be perceived as bordering on politically-incorrect... you've been warned!

A

A bit of an odd bod: A little out of the ordinary

(To) **Arse about:** To be lazy or idle

Awning over the toy-shop: Beer belly; gut

B

Back-door bandit: A gay man

Bald as a bandicoot: Bald

(She/he's a) **Bit aggro:** Aggressive

Blow a fuse: Lose one's temper

Busier than a...—VERY BUSY!
- Blue-arsed blow fly
- Blowie at a barbie/bbq
- One-armed brickie in Baghdad
- One-armed taxi driver with the crabs
- One-legged bloke in an arse kicking contest

C

Camp as a row of tents: Extremely effeminate man

Can't be arsed: Couldn't be bothered

Descriptions: Character/Personal/Emotional

(He/she) **Carked it:** Died

Could eat a horse and chase the rider: Extremely hungry

Could eat the crotch out of a low-flying duck: Extremely hungry

Crack the sads/shits: Get upset

D

(To be) **Dark on someone:** Angry

Dead to the world: Fast asleep

Deaf as a doorpost: Extremely deaf

(She/he's) **Dinky-di:** Genuine

(He/she) **Doesn't know if he/she is Arthur or Martha:** Confused

Doesn't give a bugger: Doesn't care

Done like a dinner: Completely defeated

Done like a donkey's donger: Tired

Do your…—Get angry
- Block
- Lolly
- 'nana (banana)

Aussie Talk

Don't get your knickers in a knot: Don't get upset or angry

F

Feeling a bit crook: Feeling unwell

Feeling a bit peckish: Hungry

(As) **Flat as a pancake/tack:** A woman who has little cleavage

Foaming/Frothing at the mouth: Incredibly angry

Full as a goog/boot: Have overeaten to the point where no more can be consumed; intoxicated

Full to pussy's bow: Couldn't eat another thing

G

Go crook: Get angry

Going to do your block: Going to get angry

Green around the gills: Unwell

Descriptions: Character/Personal/Emotional

H

Hair like a bush pig's arse: Hair that's impossible to manage

(As) **happy as a pig in shit:** Couldn't be happier

(As) **Happy as Larry:** Very happy (historical reference: to either the Aussie boxer, Larry Foley or shortened for 'larrikin', or hooligan)

Happy little vegemite: An Australian, generally a young one

Hasn't got a brass razoo: Poor

He's a horse hoof: rhyming slang for 'poof'—Gay man

I

I could eat the leg off a chair: I'm very hungry

In the dumps: Depressed

In a lather/tizz: Agitated; in a heightened emotional state

J

Jack/Jill of all trades: Generalist; someone able to do a lot of things reasonably well

Jumping at shadows: Edgy; nervous

K

Keen as mustard: Very keen

Kicked the bucket: Died

Knee high to a grasshopper: Very short

M

My stomach thinks my throats cut: I'm starving

O

Off your tucker: Not eating; hungry

On cloud nine: Feeling great; couldn't be better

Descriptions: Character/Personal/Emotional

P

Pack your dacks: Be scared

Packing darkies: Be scared

Pass over the great divide: Die

S

Scared the living daylights out of me: To be really scared by something

Shits me to tears: Really aggravates me

Sick as a dog: Very unwell; ill

(He/she's as) **Skinny as a rake:** Extremely thin

So thin you'd have to run around in the shower to get wet: Very slim

Spitting chips: Angry

Spit the dummy: Sudden display of anger; petulance

W

(He's/she's a bit of a) **whacker:** Someone who likes to be a bit foolish albeit in a fun way

(He's a) **wooley/wally woofter:** rhyming slang for **'poofter'**—Gay man

You've got the shits: You're angry

Sport

Australia is renowned as a nation of sports women and men, and of course, with that comes language built into our sporting culture.

Admittedly, this section is skewed towards Australian Rules Football, my own personal sporting obsession, and it's the one section I would like most to get feedback on and suggestions for so it can be broadened in scope in future editions.

A

Aerial ping-pong: AFL football

B

Bit of...—Players in a physical encounter outside the field of play
- Argy-bargy
- Biffo
- A brouhaha

Ball: Short for 'holding the ball' (AFL)

C

Chewie on your boot: Yelled at a footballer to put him off kicking a goal (AFL)

Chipping game: Where the game (AFL) is being played with small kicks (generally derogative term indicating a game that isn't very competitive or interesting)

Coathanger/To be coat-hangered: An AFL player caught high, usually around the throat

(The) **Colliwobbles:** Refers specifically to the Collingwood Football Club (AFL) falling short of winning

Sport

important games or stumbling at crucial moments in the game

Couldn't get a kick in a stampede: Aimed at a player having a bad game

Crumb gatherer/Crumber/Gathers the crumb: AFL player good at getting the loose ball

F

For mine: In my opinion

G

Given them a spray: The criticism a coach hurls at his side when they have been playing poorly

Gives him the don't argue: When a player with the ball (AFL) pushes out his hand in the direction of an opponent to fend them off and does so effectively

H

He got a few cheapies: An AFL player who has tallied a large number of game stats but who as part of this tally got some easy disposals, so hasn't played as well as the stats suggest

Have a flutter: Have a bet

Have your number taken: Reported by umpire

He kicked a sausage roll: rhyming slang for **kicked a goal**

He's a good coca cola: rhyming slang for **good bowler** (cricket)

He's got the yips: A player whose accuracy when kicking for goal is terrible

Hit in the jatz crackers: rhyming slang for 'knackers'—Taken a hit in the testicles

Hospital pass: When a player (AFL) passes the ball to a team-mate who is immediately in danger of getting bumped, crunched, or tackled with severe force—and potentially hurt—as he is put in a vulnerable position and unable to protect himself from an opposition hit

Howzat/Howizee?—What a cricketer yells in the hope he has taken a wicket

L

Low mongrel of a kick: A poor kick (AFL)

M

Mongrel worm burner: A kick along the ground that keeps low and skids along the grass (AFL, in particular a favourite of long-time personality and commentator, Rex Hunt)

N

Not much left in the tank: Players running out of energy

P

Pitch is a bunsen (burner): rhyming slang for **when a pitch (cricket) is a raging turner**

Pointy end of the season: The finals period leading up to the Grand Final

S

Sell some candy: A player (AFL) who makes a particular seemingly strategic play but fools the opponent by pretending to make a different kind of play and uses such to his advantage

(He) **Shanked it:** A player miscues a kick

Straight down the corridor: Through the middle of the ground (AFL)

Swing like a rusty gate: Poor batsman

T

Take a…—A great aerial mark (AFL)
- Hanger
- Screamer
- Speccy

Tall timber: Very tall player

That ball was a grubber: A kick (AFL) where the ball goes along the ground

They've pinged him: A player (AFL) who has been reported

Tiggy touchwood: Soft umpiring decision

Took one in the agates/plums: Hit in the testicles

W

What a grab: A great mark, usually overhead (AFL)

World of hurt: To describe how a player is feeling after he has gone down quite badly injured

At the Pub/ Social Gatherings

Lovers of sport we may be, but we also know how to balance out our more physical activities with social drinking events with friends, whether it be at the pub, a barbie at home or just about anywhere else there is a call to share a brew or two.

So, of course, there is a pool of sayings that has evolved to accompany this more relaxed 'activity'…

A

As dry as a...—Very thirsty
- Bone
- Dead dingo's donger
- Nun's box/nasty
- Pommy's towel (referring to the very clichéd 1950's idea of the English as people who did not wash often)

A man is not a camel: I need a drink

B

Been on the turps: Been drinking heavily

Bend the elbow: Have a drink

(He/she's) **Blotto:** Completely drunk

Bring a plate: Bring some food to a social gathering

C

Call ralph: Vomit

(I) **Could murder a beer:** Desperate for a beer

Crack a coldie/tinnie: Open a beer and start drinking

D

Down the hatch: Let's drink; cheers

Drinking on my Pat Malone: rhyming slang for **drinking alone**

Driving the porcelain bus: Vomiting

G

Get a black dog up ya': Let's drink; cheers (linked to 'hair of the dog' i.e. to have a drink when you have a hangover as a means of chasing the hangover away)

Going down the boozer: Going to the pub

(He/she) **Got trolleyed:** Got really drunk

(Had a) **Gut-full of piss:** Drank too much

H

Hair of the dog: An alcoholic drink to help ward off a hangover

Hit the piss/turps: Start drinking; head out to have a drink

I

I'm maggotted: So drunk you can hardly function

It's your shout: Your turn to pay for the drinks

K

Knock back a few beers: Have a couple of drinks

L

Lit up like a Christmas tree/Manly ferry: Very drunk

At the pub/Social Gatherings

M

Make mine an unleaded: Asking for a light-beer (a beer with a lower alcohol level than a standard beer)

N

Need a chunder: Need to vomit

O

Off your…—very drunk or drugged up
- Chops
- Face
- Head
- Tits
- Trolley

T

This will put hair on your chest: Big noting drinking as a man's or masculine pursuit

Talking on the porcelain telephone: Vomiting

(A) **Technicolour yawn:** Vomit

Three sheets to the wind: Drunk

(He/she's a) **Two pot screamer:** A person who gets drunk quickly

The Mating Game/ Sexology

There had to, of course, be a section on sex and the mating game, and with it comes a warning of a different kind to earlier sections—some of the language is a little 'risque'—the section is about sex, after all, so it's unavoidable, right?

Only read on if you aren't too easily offended...

A

All dolled up/tizzed up: A woman who has dressed up to impress

All over him/her like a rash: Not afraid to show someone you are attracted to them

Angle of the dangle: Comment about whether you have an erection

A bun in the oven: Pregnant

B

(She's) **Banged up:** Pregnant

(He/she) **bangs like a dunny door (in the wind):** Promiscuous

(She/he is a) **bit of alright:** Quite attractive

(Have you been) **Buffin' the muffin?:** Masturbating

C

Crack a fat: Get an erection

Cut your grass (grass cutter)/Cut your lunch: When someone steals or moves in on your love or lust interest

D

Dip the wick: Had sexual intercourse

Do the dirty: Have sexual intercourse

Drilling for vegemite: Having anal sex

F

(To) **Feed the chooks:** Masturbate

(You're/I'm) **Feeling clucky:** Wanting to have a child

(He's) **Flogging the log:** Masturbating

G

Get on/Pash on with someone: To kiss (usually French kiss)

Give someone the flick: Break off a relationship

H

Have your beer goggles on: Questioning someone's judgement as being below their usual standards in terms of a person they slept with or hit on when they were drunk

Have a perve: Sexually appraise someone

He's a sly butcher: Someone who likes to have anal sex (i.e. 'he sneaks his meat in through the back door')

Horizontal lambada: Sexual intercourse

Hot to trot: Someone who is acting lustily

I

If you've got the time, I've got the place: Standard pick-up line

J

Jerkin' the gherkin: Masturbating

L

Let's play hide the sausage: Sexual intercourse

Like a bowling ball down Bourke St: A woman who has a lot of sex and as a result is regarded as 'loose' metaphorically, in terms of her lasciviousness, and literally in terms of how regular sex has 'loosened' up her sex organs!

M

Map of Tassie: The shape of the female pubic mound as resembling a map of the state of Tasmania, Australia

M

Meat and two veg: Penis and testicles

O

(The) **One-eyed trouser snake:** Penis

S

She's had more pricks than a second-hand dartboard: A loose woman

She's on high beam: A woman whose nipples are erect when aroused (or cold!)

(He's) **Shooting blanks:** A male's impotence or inability to have children

Spearing the bearded clam: Sexual intercourse

T

Tart yourself up: Get dressed up for a night out

Tickle the ivories: French kissing

(As) **Toey as a roman sandal:** Wanting some kind of sexual release

U

Unbutton the mutton: To reveal one's penis; also to urinate

Up the duff: Pregnant

W

Wanna root?—Rough and ready pick up line

Welcome mat: The patch of hair above someone's buttocks at the base of the spine

Whats cookin' good lookin'?—Classic pick-up line

Who's thinking of the mantle-piece when you're stoking the fire?—A woman's breast size is of less interest, or not so important, to a man when a couple are having intercourse

Y

You can see what she's had for breakfast: A woman sitting with her legs wide open in an unlady-like fashion

Toilet Humour

Going to the toilet or restroom or bathroom or whatever you care to call it is obviously a simple fact of life.

In its most basic form, we might refer to our visit to the 'loo' as going to do 'number ones' or 'number twos', but there are plenty of other more 'descriptive' ways of indicating that one needs to be excused to perform one kind of ablution or another.

Similar to previous sections, there are sayings that might mildly offend or be a little too much for the more sensitive, so read on if you dare…

A

A bit more choke and you would have started: To break wind loudly

B

Bad case of the trots: Diarrhoea

Brown-eyed mullet: Faeces floating in the ocean

C

Chuck a browneye: To drop your underpants and flash your bum

D

Drain the lizard: Urinate

Drop the kids off at the pool: Defecate

Drop your guts: To break wind

G

Going to drain the one-eyed trouser snake: Urinate

Going to shake hands with the unemployed: Urinate

H

Have a/Need to/ Take a slash: Urinate

N

Need to drain the man vein: Urinate

Need to strangle a brownie: Defecate

P

Point percy at the porcelain: Urinate

Pushing cloth/Touching cotton: Very close to needing to defecate

S

Shake hands with the unemployed: Urinate

Shake hands with the wife's best friend: Urinate

Strain the potatoes: Urinate

Strangle/Give birth to a politician: Defecate

Syphon the python: Urinate

T

Take a slash: Urinate

Take the kids to the pool/Drop the kids off at the pool: Need to defecate

(Take a) **Team trot:** Urinate in a group, usually men

There's a brown dog barking at the back door: Urgent need to defecate

W

Water the horse: Urinate

Who opened their lunch?—Who broke wind?

Time and Space

Australia's wide open spaces tend to skew sayings about geography and other spatial references to refer to long distances or places far away from the major urban centres.

In terms of time, the 'she'll be right' mate mentality might be construed as making Australians a little lackadaisical when it comes to time-keeping.

A

A freckle past a hair: Standard response if asked the time and you don't have a watch

Any tick of the clock: Soon

Apple Islanders: Residents of Tasmania (the shape of the State of Tasmania, the island located in the far south of the continent, has been likened to an apple and Tasmania was once one of the largest apple producers in the world)

B

(The) **Back blocks:** Somewhere far away

Back of Bourke: A remote area

Back of Beyond: Outback Australia

Banana bender: A resident of Queensland (located in northern Australia where tropical weather means bananas grow in abundance)

Beer o'clock: End of the work day and time for a drink

C

Cockroaches: Residents of New South Wales (possible origins are either from the fact that more humid weather in NSW means the existence of cockroaches is widespread; also the nickname of the NSW Rugby side)

Croweater: A resident of South Australian (originally people from Western Australia were referred to as 'croweaters'); the term is believed to originate from 19th century rumours that when times got tough in South Australia, locals literally ate crows to bring meat into their diets)

D

Duck up/Nick up/Pop up the street: Head somewhere close by, usually to perform some task or errand

G

Go across/up/down the road: Head out to run some errands

Gotta get up at Dawn's crack: Need to rise early

H

Haven't seen you in yonks: Not seen you in a long time (also a greeting)

I

In the middle of Woop Woop: Very remote

In two shakes of a lamb's tail: Soon

In just a jiffy: In a moment; give me a moment

J

Just down the road: Close by

M

Mexicans: Residents of Victoria (because it is south of the USA border, similar to Mexico being south of the NSW border); veiled reference to Victorians being somehow inferior to New South Welshmen

N

No one within cooee: A remote and uninhabited area with few inhabitants

Not within a bull's roar: Nowhere nearby

O

Off the beaten track: Well away from civilisation

Out in the sticks: In the remote outback

S

Sandgropers: Residents of West Australia (presumably due to how much sand there is in Australia's largest and most remote region that takes up a vast chunk of the Western side of the continent)

South of the border: Victoria, a state in the lower south of the Australian continent (see also 'Mexicans' reference)

U

Up at a sparrow's fart: Early

W

Waiting till the cows come home: Waiting for a long time

Within cooee of here: Somewhere relatively close; to 'cooee' is to call out in a particularly Aussie bushman's way, so to be within cooee is to be close enough to hear that shout

Online Acronyms

The virtual world is increasingly encroaching on 'normal' life to such a degree that a unique language is developing to facilitate conversation in online spaces—short, sharp, to the point and, usually, fairly obvious.

Because the online sphere is an international environment, most of the language developing out of it is generic and non-country specific.

Regardless, this collection would be incomplete without a selection of Internet Acronym slang that are steadily becoming the language of the 'interwebs'.

Aussie Talk

BBS—Be back soon

BFF—Best friends forever

BRB—Be right back

BS—Bullshit

G2G—Got to go

JK—Just kidding

LMAO—Laughing my arse off

LOL—Laugh out loud; lots of love

NP—No problems

NQR—Not quite right

OMG—Oh my god

OTT—Over the top

ROFL—Rolling on the floor laughing

STFU—Shut the f*ck up

TMI—Too much information

TTFN—Ta-ta for now

TTYL—Talk to you later

WDYT—What do you think?

WTF—What the f*ck?!

General: All the rest!

Aussie slang and sayings are so liberally used by Australians that there exists a body of sayings that defy categorisation.

This made it necessary to include a more general section, and a quite long one at that, to ensure that some classic Aussie slanguage didn't get left out.

A

A change is as good as a holiday: An optimistic and supportive response to someone who is making some kind of change to their normal life

A dead cert: Something that is 100 per cent sure of happening

(To) **Add insult to injury:** To make matters worse

(It's) **All the go:** Very popular

All dressed up with nowhere to go: To be prepared for something that wont happen

All over it like a rash: Ready to get something done; have already sorted something out ahead of expectation

Any old Joe blow could tell you: Indicating that the information is common knowledge

Argue the toss: Disagree with the decision

Arse about face: Something arranged in an odd way

Arse over tit: Upside down; head over heels; the wrong orientation

As much chance as pushing shit up a hill: No chance at all

General: All the rest!

B

(A) **Bag of fruit:** rhyming slang for **a suit**

(Your/my) **Bag of strife/trouble and strife:** rhyming slang for **wife**

Bail somebody up: To corner somebody physically

Barking up the wrong tree: Assuming the wrong thing; making the wrong judgement about a situation or person

Beat around the bush: Avoid the topic

Between, you, me and the gatepost: Urging someone to keep the information you are about to tell them private

Better than a ham sandwich: Better than nothing

Better than a poke in the eye with a burnt stick: It could be worse

Big note yourself: Make more of yourself than actually merits

Bit of a kerfuffle: Something of a disturbance

Bite the bullet: Get on with something despite the consequences

(The) **Blind leading the blind:** Two people trying to do something, with neither having any real idea as to how to do it

Boots 'n all: Wholeheartedly

Bottom of the harbour scheme: Sly business practice that helps avoid tax

Bringing home the bacon: Supplying income, generally to a family

Bust a boiler: Work too hard at something

Bust a foofer valve: Too over-exert one-self physically ('foofer', referring to heart)

C

Call a spade a spade: Not hide from the facts; tell it like it is

Call it a day: Finish up

Can I get a dink?—Can you give me a ride on the back of your bike?

Can't take a trick: A person who experiences one piece of bad luck after another

General: All the rest!

Catch some ZZZZZs: Get some sleep

Cat got your tongue?—Questioning someone's silence with a sense of suspicion about why they are being silent or not forthcoming with some information

Charge like a wounded bull: Overcharge for something

Chew the fat: Discuss something at length

Chief cook and bottle washer: Someone who takes on a lot of responsibilities

Chockers: Very full, usually in reference to a place filled with people

To Chuck a...—Oft used term used in place of the verb 'to do'
- Mental—Get angry
- Sickie—Take a day off work due to feigned illness
- Spaz—Have a temper tantrum
- U-ie—Perform a u-turn while driving
- Wobbly—Get angry
- Yonnie—Throw a stone out across water

Clutching at spanners: A twist on 'clutching at straws'—To unreasonably hope for or believe something

Cock and bull story: A lie

General: All the rest!

Cold...—Freezing
- As a witch's tit
- Enough to freeze the balls off a brass monkey
- Enough to freeze the nuts off a tractor

Come a cropper/gutser: Have an accident; to fail at something

Come on slow coach: Hurry up

Cook the books: To interfere with calculations or accounting practices in an effort to be deceptive and make a gain

Cooking with gas: Making headway with a task; getting a lot done

Cop it on the chin: Take responsibility for something

Cop it sweet: Get lucky

Copped one in the nurries/plums: Hit in the testicles

Couldn't be done in a month of Sundays: Something near-impossible

D

Dead as...—Self-explanatory
- A dodo

- A donkey's (donger)
- A doornail
- Mutton chops

(I) **Didn't come down in the last shower:** Don't try to deceive me; don't underestimate my intelligence

Didn't even get a guernsey: Didn't get any recognition

Didn't bat an eyelid: Didn't take any notice

(To) **Dob on someone:** To report someone's behaviour as being improper (school term)

Doing a roaring trade: Very busy, usually in a commercial sense

Don't believe everything you hear: Questioning the veracity of something

Down the gurgler: Wasted

(At the) **Drop of a hat:** Any excuse

Drop your bundle: Stop trying

F

Fart arse around: Not get anything done; procrastinate

General: All the rest!

Fighting like two cats in a sugar bag: A woman not wearing a bra

Five finger(ed) discount: Stolen goods

Flogging a dead horse: Persisting with something when it's pointless

(A bit of) **Froth and bubble:** Useless chatter about something that has no real import

Fly the Aussie flag: In public with shirt hanging out

For love or money: No matter what

G

Give it the flick: Dispose of something

Get on like a house on fire: Have a great relationship

Get the axe: Be sacked from employment; to lose a placing of some kind or position

Get the drift: Understand

Gets the job done: Something that is touch and go but work nonetheless

Get your back up: Get defensive

Give a gob-full: Verbally abuse

Aussie Talk

Give it a bash/a burl/a red-hot go: Try something with gusto

Give it a butcher's: rhyming slang for **take a look**

Give it/someone the flick: Let go of something or someone

Give me the good oil: Tell me the news or gossip

Give someone heaps: Make fun of someone

Go/Gone troppo: Gone crazy (troppo referring to the 'tropics')

Going like hotcakes: Selling very fast

Got some mail: Have heard some news or gossip

Give someone mate's rates: Offering a discount for a service or goods

Give someone a leg up: Help someone

Give you a bell: Call someone on the phone

Give you the shis/irits: Irritate you

Given the arse: Sacked; relationship terminated

Glutton for punishment: Someone who, by their own actions, makes things worse in their life or works too hard

Go for broke: Try really hard

General: All the rest!

Go through you like a dose of salts: Something that happens very quickly

Going through a purple patch: Experiencing a dream run when everything is perfect in one's life

Going to see a man about a dog: Used to avoid telling someone your actual destination

Good as gold: As good as can be

Got me by the short and curlies: Said by someone who has been caught doing something they shouldn't; to get caught red-handed

(She's/he's) **Got Nunn and Buckley's:** That person has no chance at all

H

Have a Bex and a lie down: Remedy for everything; can indicate that it is time to get calm and just slow down or pull back from a precarious situation

Have a bo-peep: To take a sly look at something

Have a crack: Try it

Have/Give us a gander: Let me see

(He/she's) **having a Barry Crocker:** rhyming slang for 'shocker'—Someone in trouble or having a particularly bad run of luck at that moment (often used in sport)

Have a lend of someone: Not telling someone the truth

Have a squiz/sticky beak: Have a look

Have a yabber/yarn: Have a conversation

Have the wood on someone: Holding some kind of power or sway over someone, often used in sport

Haven't got two bob to rub together: Have no money

Having a blue: An argument

He gave me an earful: To be berated for something

General: All the rest!

Hole in the wall: Automatic teller machine

Home and hosed: In a winning position; almost finished

Horses for courses: Each to their own

How long is a piece of string?—I can't answer your question

I

I'll go and take a Captain Cook: rhyming slang for **I'll look**

I'm humping my bluey: Carrying a swag; carrying your life on your back

In the bag: As good as mine; something almost completed but it may as well be given how close it is to completion or success

In the altogether: Naked

Is it ridgey didge?—Authentic

It was the last time I looked: Throwaway general response

It's a boomerang: I want what I'm lending to you back

It's a piece of piss: Easy

It's gone walkabout: I have no idea where it is; it's missing

J

(The) **Jury is still out:** No decision has been made yet

K

Keep your ear to the ground: Try and find out for me

Knocked off work: Finished work

Know a thing or two: I know more than I appear to or than I'm letting on

General: All the rest!

L

Led up the garden path: Easily convinced; fooled

Life wasn't meant to be easy (George Bernard Shaw, via Malcolm Fraser)—Said in response to someone complaining

Lift your game: Try harder

Like a shag on a rock: Obvious

Like shit off a shovel: Quickly

Like the clappers: Quickly

M

Make a quid: Earn some money

More bang for your buck: Better value

More than you can poke a stick at: A large number or quantity

N

Need to go to the fang carpenter: Must see the dentist

Need to have a chinwag: Need to talk

Aussie Talk

Nose down bum up: Working hard

Not a patch on: Nowhere near as good as

Not going to have a bar of: Don't want anything to do with something or situation

Nut something out: Work hard at understanding some thing or situation

On a good wicket: Things are going well; you are in a good position

He/she's on big bikkies: Earning good money

O

On your Pat Malone: rhyming slang for **all alone**

On for young and old: Describing a situation that is difficult to stop; the absence of restraint

On the blink: Not working properly

On the outer: Unpopular

P

Pay through the nose: Pay an exorbitant amount

Pipped at the post: Just beaten

General: All the rest!

Playing possum: Pretending

Pull up stumps: Finish something; cut ties

Pushing shit uphill: Working at something that is nigh impossible

Put in the hard yards: Done the strong foundational work needed to achieve something

Put in your two bob's worth: Have your say

Put it on the never never: Pay for something on credit or account

Put the boot in: Make a bad situation worse

Put the hard word on: Put pressure on; ask forcefully for something

Put the mozz on: To hex or put a curse on someone

Put the wind up you: Warn you

R

Raining cats and dogs: Heavy rain

Right up your alley: Exactly what you want

Rock up: Arrive

Rough end of the stick/pineapple: Someone who

finds themselves in a particularly difficult situation or to whom fate has been unkind

Run rings around: Far superior

Running on empty: Close to not being able to continue with or complete some endeavour

S

Scarce as hen's teeth: Very rare

Shit before the shovel: Joking way of telling someone they can go before you

Shot through like a Bondi tram: Disappeared or left quickly

Show you the ropes: Teach you something

Shower, shit and shave: Get ready to go somewhere

Sink the boot in: To vehemently verbally attack someone

Sitting on the fence: Being indecisive; remaining impartial

Six of one, half dozen of the other: Not too much either way; expressing difficulty on deciding or adjudicating something

General: All the rest!

(Something is a bit) **Skew whiff or iffy:** Something is slightly odd

Spread like wildfire: Happen very quickly

Strapped for cash: Low on cash

Suck it and see: Try something you haven't tried before and see what happens; take a risk

T

Take a piece out of: Hurt someone

Take a punt: Have a try

Take a shine to: Find to one's liking

Take a smoko: Have a break

Take a squizz: Look at something

Take the bull by the horns: Seize control

Taken to the cleaners: Lost everything (usually financial)

Talk the leg off an iron pot: Someone who talks too much

That was a piece of cake: Easy

Things are crook in Tallarook: A bad situation

Turn up for the books: That wasn't expected

U

Up and down like a bride's nightie: Indecisive

Up shit creek without a paddle: In a lot of trouble

Up the spout: In trouble

W

We had a barney: A fight

Went down like a cup of cold sick: News not taken very well

Went for a sixer: Fell over

What a dag: Term of endearment for a slightly clumsy, nerdy or uncool person

What a kerfuffle': Commotion

General: All the rest!

What do you do for a crust?— What is your job?

Whatever floats your boat: Whatever makes you happy

What's that got to do with the price of fish?— That is irrelevant

What's the damage?—How much does it cost?; what do I owe?

When push comes to shove: When there is no alternative

When the shit hits the fan: When news gets out, there will be trouble

Won it by a bee's dick: Only just won something

Won't have a bar of him/her/that: Don't want anything to do with a person or something

Wouldn't know him from a bar of soap: Have no idea who that person is

Wrap your laughing gear around this: Taste this

Y

You got ants in your pants: You're jittery

Your better half: Your partner or spouse

Your cheque is in the mail: Stop worrying, you'll get paid

Your shout: Your turn to pay

You're such a worry wart: You are too concerned

ORDER

AUSSIE TALK

Paul Bugeja

		Qty
ISBN 9781922036834		
RRP	AU$17.99	.....
Postage within Australia	AU$5.00	.....
	TOTAL* $_____	
	* All prices include GST	

Name:..

Address: ....

....

Phone:...

Email: ....

Payment: ❏ Money Order ❏ Cheque ❏ MasterCard ❏ Visa

Cardholders Name:..

Credit Card Number: ....

Signature:...

Expiry Date: ....

Allow 7 days for delivery.

Payment to: Marzocco Consultancy (ABN 14 067 257 390)
PO Box 12544
A'Beckett Street, Melbourne, 8006
Victoria, Australia
admin@brolgapublishing.com.au

Be Published

Publish through a successful Australian publisher.
Brolga Publishing is represented through:
- **National** book trade distribution, including sales, marketing & distribution through **Macmillan Australia**.
- **International** book trade distribution to
    - The United Kingdom
    - North America
    - Sales representation in South East Asia
- **Worldwide e-Book distribution**

For details and inquiries, contact:
Brolga Publishing Pty Ltd
PO Box 12544
A'Beckett St VIC 8006

Phone: 0414 608 494
admin@brolgapublishing.com.au
markzocchi@brolgapublishing.com.au
ABN: 46 063 962 443
(Email for a catalogue request)